CIPS STUDY

G000152281

PROFESSIONAL ~~DIPLOMA IN~~
PROCUREMENT AND SUPPLY

REVISION NOTES

Corporate and business strategy

© Profex Publishing Limited, 2012

Printed and distributed by:
The Chartered Institute of Purchasing & Supply, Easton House, Easton on the Hill, Stamford,
Lincolnshire PE9 3NZ
Tel: +44 (0) 1780 756 777
Fax: +44 (0) 1780 751 610
Email: info@cips.org
Website: www.cips.org

First edition November 2012

Contents

Preface

Welcome to your Revision Notes.

Your Revision Notes are a summarised version of the material contained in your Course Book. If you find that the Revision Notes refer to material that you do not recollect clearly, you should refer back to the Course Book to refresh your memory.

There is space at the end of each chapter in your Revision Notes where you can enter your own notes for reference.

A note on style

Throughout your Study Packs you will find that we use the masculine form of personal pronouns. This convention is adopted purely for the sake of stylistic convenience – we just don't like saying 'he/she' all the time. Please don't think this reflects any kind of bias or prejudice.

November 2012

CHAPTER 1

Strategy and Strategic Decisions

What is strategy?

Johnson, Scholes & Whittington define strategy as 'the direction and scope of an organisation over the long term, which achieves advantage in a changing environment through its configuration of resources and competencies, with the aim of fulfilling stakeholder expectations.' This definition highlights several characteristics of strategic decisions.

- They relate to the **scope of the organisation**.
- They will influence the direction of the organisation in the **long term**.
- They are normally about trying to achieve **competitive advantage**.
- They attempt to match the organisation's activities to the demands of its dynamic **environment** and the potential of its **resources and competencies**.
- They will be influenced by **stakeholder** values and expectations.

Strategic decisions are likely: to be complex in nature; to be made in situations where the future is uncertain; to affect operational decisions; to demand an integrated, cross-functional approach; to involve relationships with outside organisations; to involve change.

Ohmae's strategic triangle or Three Cs model: corporation based strategy; customer-based strategy; competitor-based strategy.

Mintzberg's perspectives on strategy (Five Ps): plan; ploy; pattern; position; perspective.

Strategic decision-making encompasses a wide number of elements.

- Expressing the organisation's vision of its desired future state ('strategic intent')
- Determining the scope and boundaries of the organisation's activities
- Relating the organisation's activities to the environment
- Matching the organisation's activities to its resources and capabilities
- Sourcing, mobilising, allocating and re-allocating resources
- Influencing the long-term direction of the organisation
- Providing a guiding and constraining framework for operational decisions
- Reflecting the values and expectations of powerful individuals, coalitions and stakeholders
- Defining the organisation's need for, and orientation to, change.

The vocabulary of strategy

TERM	DEFINITION/COMMENTS	EXAMPLE
Mission	A general expression of the overall purpose of the organisation	Provide all customers with access to quality products
Vision (strategic intent)	An expression of the desired future state of the organisation	Provide best value for money in the market
Values	Core beliefs and qualities valued by the organisation	Zero waste, cost-focused, value-adding, fair and responsible pricing
Goal	A general, often qualitative, statement of aim or purpose, in line with the mission	Achieve lowest cost responsible supply
Objective	A more quantified, specific statement of what needs to be achieved over a given period of time.	Reduce external spend by 30% over five years
Scope	A statement of the organisation's scope in three dimensions.	Externalise logistics, transport and warehouse management
Strategic capability (or competitive strengths)	Resources and competencies that can be used to create and deliver customer value and competitive advantage.	Well-developed partnership agreements with suppliers with lean supply capability
Strategies	Broad statements about the long-term direction of the organisation	Low-cost country sourcing
Business model	The structure of business processes to deliver strategies	Lean supply
Control	Monitoring progress and results to assess the effectiveness of strategies and implementation	Monitor cost-saving initiatives and cost savings

Strategic management

Operational management is essentially concerned with the effective and efficient management and control of resources already deployed; often in a limited part of the organisation; within the context of an existing strategy; involving detailed planning and analysis; over a short to medium time horizon.

Strategic management is essentially concerned with the development of resources and the direction of the enterprise; managing complexity in uncertain and non-routine situations; with organisation-wide scope, covering a number of different operational areas (finance, IT, marketing and so on); at a high, broad level; over a long time horizon.

Strategic decisions affect operational decisions.

- The successful achievement of strategic plans depends on the alignment (fit or congruence) and effectiveness of operational plans and activities.

- The resource-based view of strategy emphasises that real strategic advantage can be achieved at the operational level.

Mary Coulter defines strategic management as: 'a series of steps in which organisational members analyse the current situation, decide on strategies, put those strategies into action, and evaluate, modify or change strategies as needed'. This definition reflects an influential three-stage approach to strategic management familiar to generations of students from the work of Johnson, Scholes and Whittington: analysis of the strategic position of the organisation (P), choice of strategic options for the future (C) and turning strategies into action (A).

According to Johnson, Scholes & Whittington, 'strategic analysis is concerned with understanding the strategic position of the organisation in terms of its external environment, internal resources and competencies, and the expectations and influences of stakeholders'.

Strategic choice 'involves understanding the underlying bases for future strategy at both the business unit and corporate levels, and the options for developing strategy in terms of both the directions and methods of development'. This effectively subdivides this stage of the process into two phases: identify the possible bases on which to construct a strategy; generate strategic options.

The third stage of the strategic management process is strategy implementation, which 'is concerned with the translation of strategy into organisational action through organisational structure and design, resource planning and the management of strategic change'.

Strategic management in context

General principles of strategic management apply to most or all organisations, regardless of the sector in which they operate. However, the emphasis on particular aspects of strategic management is likely to differ from one organisation to another.

The issue of business purpose and scope is less important in the context of small businesses because of the limited nature of the organisation's activities. Strategy is likely to be strongly (and often informally) led by top managers or owners and strategy development may be limited by their values, experience, competencies and expectations.

Issues of competitive pressure are likely to be very important, because typically a small business may be just one of many servicing a particular sector. (Though this is not the case for all small businesses, some of which are 'niche' providers.) Key strategic concerns are likely to be establishing a customer base or competitive niche, raising finance and (in entrepreneurial style) exploiting opportunities for growth.

Small businesses are likely to have difficulties in raising substantial sums of capital, which means that the range of strategic choice may be limited.

The traditional divide between organisations in the manufacturing and service sectors appears far less significant in an era of world class practices. For the purposes of strategic management, it is preferable to think of the output offered by a service organisation as just another kind of 'product'. Despite this, there remain important differences in emphasis between the two sectors

Public sector organisations include nationalised companies, government agencies, health services and many more. The element of competition is a key factor distinguishing private sector organisations from those in the public sector. It would be a mistake to assume that competition does not exist in the public sector, but it often takes the form of competition with other public sector organisations for scarce resources controlled by, for example, the central government. Political ideology and policy is a key factor in establishing the mission and objectives of public sector organisations.

Perhaps the key strategic characteristic in relation to public-sector organisations is the need to satisfy a more diverse group of stakeholders, including those who provide funding and those who 'consume' the services provided.

OWN NOTES

OWN NOTES

CHAPTER 2

Levels of Strategy

Levels of strategy

Strategic plans vary in the level at which they are taken, the breadth of the business they cover, the detail they examine and the length of their horizon.

- Corporate strategies apply to the whole organisation. They focus on the broad, general direction of the organisation, and how value will be added, over the long term (say, 3–5 years).
- Tactical or business level strategies apply to particular divisions, functions or strategic business units. They focus on the tasks and objectives required to pursue the chosen corporate strategies and compete successfully in particular markets, over the medium term (say, 1–2 years).
- Operational strategies and plans apply to functions and departments. They focus on the specific detail of tasks, targets, resources and actions needed to deliver the corporate and business level strategies, over the short term (up to a year, say).

A **strategic business unit** is 'a part of an organisation for which there is a distinct external market for goods or services that is different from another part or SBU'.

Global strategy (arguably another 'level of strategy') has been defined as the search for competitive advantage outside an organisation's domestic borders.

Most writers agree with the idea that there is a hierarchy of objectives in organisations, just as there is a hierarchy of managers. The objectives at the top of the hierarchy are relevant to all aspects and members of the organisation, at a general level; they cascade down to the more specific objectives of business units, groups and individuals. The terms commonly given to the statement of objectives at each stage of this cascade are: mission; goals; objectives; strategy; tactics; operational plans.

Corporate strategy and objectives

Vision is defined as 'strategic intent, or the desired future state of the organisation... an aspiration around which a strategist, perhaps a chief executive, might seek to focus the attention and energies of members of the organisation'. Three elements of corporate vision: a sense of direction; a sense of discovery; a sense of destiny.

The mission of an organisation is a broad definition of the purpose of the organisation: what business are we in? what are we trying to achieve? The organisation's mission statement is usually a brief statement of the purpose, business areas and key cultural values of the organisation, stated in qualitative rather than quantitative terms. Its purpose is primarily to communicate a sense of meaning and direction to the people inside the organisation, as a guideline for activity.

Goals and objectives transform the mission or vision into targets or aims which the organisation will pursue. The terms are often used interchangeably, but it may be helpful to think of goals as statements of a desired future state ('where we want to get to'), and objectives as more specific, time-assigned, quantified targets to pursue in order to achieve each goal ('what we need to do to get there'). Effective objectives are SMART.

Common corporate objectives

For private sector business organisations, the primary corporate objective is often financial in nature: examples include profitability, return on capital employed or earnings per share.

Possible secondary objectives:

- Market share
- Market position or standing
- Brand value and positioning
- Product development
- Technology and innovation
- Human resource management
- Corporate social responsibility and ethics

Attention to **profitability** does not necessarily imply an objective of *profit maximisation*.

Market share is a key indicator of performance for many private sector organisations in competitive markets. It enables firms to identify whether increases in their sales result from the market expanding – or from their capturing customers and sales from competitors.

The aim of profitability is to generate a return on the **value of shareholders' investment** of capital in the business, in the form of: dividends; growth in capital.

Ethical issues may affect organisations at three basic levels: at the macro level; at the corporate level; and at the individual level.

CSR describes a wide range of obligations that an organisation may feel it has towards the society in which it operates: its 'secondary' stakeholders. CSR is increasingly prioritised as a corporate objective in the private sector, because of public, media and consumer pressure, and the risk of reputational damage as a result of the exposure of irresponsible corporate (and supply chain) behaviour. This is despite the argument of Friedman and Sternberg that 'the social responsibility of business is profit maximisation'.

Strategic alignment

If an organisation is to achieve its corporate and strategic change objectives, the plans set for each unit and function must be co-ordinated with each other so that they contribute towards the overall objectives. This is sometimes referred to as 'goal congruence'.

Vertical alignment means ensuring that the goal of every activity contributes towards the overall or higher objectives of the business.

Horizontal alignment is about ensuring that the plans of every unit in an organisation are co-ordinated with those of others, so that they work effectively together.

One of the key consequences of the alignment concept is that the vision and objectives for strategic change must be 'sold' downward to contributing units and individuals, in order to secure co-operation or 'buy in'.

The 7S framework

Elements in the 7S framework:

- **Strategy** is a chosen course of action leading to the allocation of the firm's resources over time in order to reach defined goals
- **Structure** refers to the formal organisation structure
- **Systems** refer to procedures, tools and processes that standardise work and information flow in the organisation
- **Staff** are the human resources of the organisation
- **Style** refers to corporate image, organisation culture and management style
- **Skills** refer to the distinctive capabilities of key personnel or of the organisation as a whole
- **Shared values** are the underlying guiding beliefs and assumptions that shape the way the organisation sees itself and its purpose.

All the elements are interlinked: altering any one variable will have an effect on the others and on the whole.

Corporate objectives and the supply chain

In recent decades, the role performed by procurement and supply chain functions has generally become less administrative or clerical, and has taken on a more strategic aspect. Reasons for this:

- Changes in the cost base of manufacturing companies
- Adoption of world class manufacturing techniques
- Increased importance of quality management
- Need to develop strategic collaborative supply relationships
- Need for proactive corporate risk management

It is imperative for procurement and supply chain strategies to align with business and corporate strategies: firstly, to support and enable their achievement (by securing the right resources at the right place at the right time at the right price); and secondly, to justify and reinforce purchasing's strategic role and contribution.

Links between corporate and supply chain functional objectives

CORPORATE OBJECTIVES	PROCUREMENT AND SUPPLY CHAIN OBJECTIVES
Maintain and increase market share	Provide supplies to match customer needs; assure quality; reduce delivery lead time; reduce cost
Improve profits, cashflow, and return on capital	Reduce stocks; improve reliability; more frequent deliveries
Shorten time to market	Early supplier involvement; simultaneous engineering
Eliminate non-core activities	Develop effective make-or-buy policy; integrate sourcing, procurement and capacity planning
Introduce continuous improvement	Optimise the supplier base; partnership and co-makership approaches; reduce product complexity; increase accuracy and reliability
Become world class supplier	Work with suppliers to establish world class standards; improve flexibility of response to market conditions; liaison with technological sources

The functional strategies of procurement and supply can contribute to a number of key corporate objectives: quality; cost reduction and control; innovation; delivery and service levels; CSR and sustainability.

Various formal and informal processes may be implemented to ensure that supply chain strategies are integrated with corporate strategy.

- A formal long-term procurement and supply chain plan may be developed as part of the corporate planning process.
- Procurement and supply chain managers may be involved in the corporate planning process.
- The main board of directors may act as an integrating mechanism.
- Interpersonal relations between supply chain managers and a supportive chief executive may informally facilitate integration.

In the technical sense, the term **supply chain management** (or SCM) has been given to a particular strategic approach which recognises the interdependent nature of supply issues, and what Saunders calls 'the systemic nature of supply activities, as captured by such phrases as "supply chains", "value systems", "networks" and "extended enterprises".'

SCM consists primarily of building **co-operative relationships** across the supply chain, so that the whole chain works together to add value for the end customer in a profitable, risk-managed and competitive way.

A strategic SCM approach thus implies the need to develop strategies for:

- The role and positioning (or repositioning) of an organisation within the total supply chain (eg through forward or backward integration)
- The configuration of the chain or network, and the competitive or collaborative nature of the relationships within it
- The selection of strategic supply chain partners
- Internal and trans-organisational processes for materials and information flow
- Collaborative and integrative arrangements where appropriate.

The goals of a strategic SCM approach:

- Reducing non-value-adding (waste) activities throughout the supply chain
- Reducing cycle times
- Improving responsiveness to customer requirements
- Giving access to complementary resources and capabilities
- Enhancing quality and service
- Improving supply chain communication
- Reducing total costs
- Optimising the balance of service levels and costs

Limitations of SCM:

- There must be sufficient resources and systems in place to develop suppliers effectively.
- The investment in integrated systems, supplier development and so on may not be worth the quality and cost gains for a given organisation.
- Increased collaboration and integration may expose the firm to risks.
- SCM, as a radical strategic shift, requires both internal support and supplier willingness.
- Network information sharing may expose the firm to loss of informational and intellectual assets and distinctive competencies.
- It is difficult to measure the effectiveness of (or business case for) SCM co-operation in meaningful ways.
- There may be problems in fairly distributing the gains and risks of co-operation among supply chain partners

OWN NOTES

CHAPTER 3

Developing Strategy

Intended and emergent strategy

Two views of strategy development:

- The **intended strategy** view (also known as the rational or design view) argues that strategies are intentionally developed as a result of strategic intent, and rational analysis and planning processes carried out by senior management.
- The **emergent strategy** view argues that strategies do not always come about as the result of intentional management planning, but tend to 'emerge' or take shape in an organisation over time.

Mintzberg's alternatives to formal strategic planning:

- **Opportunistic** (or **entrepreneurial) strategies.** An organisation may take advantage of changes in the environment or recognise the potential of new skills or technology in an opportunistic manner, or an entrepreneur may have a vision for an opportunity in the market place.
- **Imposed strategies**, where choice is constrained by environmental pressures and imperatives, or by powerful external stakeholders.
- **Emergent strategies**, which are 'formed' (rather than being deliberately formulated) through various processes: 'One idea leads to another until a new pattern forms.'

Realised strategy is the strategy that is actually followed by the organisation in practice. This may *not* be the same as the intended or planned strategy, because strategies may be imposed, or may emerge, in various ways.

Moreover, not all *intended* strategies become *realised* (or achieved) strategies: in other words, the strategy may be **unrealised.**

Strategic leadership

'An organisation's strategy may be influenced by strategic leaders: individuals (or perhaps a small group of individuals) whose personality, position or reputation gives them dominance over the strategy development process.'

A range of approaches to strategic leadership – leaders may focus on:

- Their strategic role (the strategy approach)
- Developing people (the human assets approach)

- Developing 'core competencies' in the organisation (the expertise approach).
- Controlling organisational performance, ensuring efficiency of processes and predictability of outputs (the control approach).
- Their role as change champions or drivers (the change approach).

Supply chain strategic leadership: one of the key functions of leaders in procurement and supply is to lead (as well as manage) the supply chain.

- Motivating and inspiring supply chain partners
- Utilising motivational and relationship-maintaining influencing approaches
- Mobilising and developing resources and capabilities within the supply chain
- Introducing changes in a constructive manner
- Facilitating collaboration and alliance-building between stakeholders
- Leading by example in desired standards of conduct and performance
- Utilising influence to encourage the raising of standards

Strategic planning

Strategic planning involves systematic, step-by-step procedures for developing organisational strategy. The rational or strategic planning model (aiming for intended strategy) assumes that the organisation takes a structured, formal approach to its development and direction.

- Strategies result from a controlled, conscious process of formal planning, divided into distinct steps, each supported by techniques
- Responsibility for the process rests with senior management and staff planners
- Strategies are made explicit so that they can be implemented through detailed attention to objectives, budgets, programs and operating plans of various kinds.

Bryson put forward a model (the **strategy change cycle**) designed to be orderly *and* dynamic (nonlinear, fluid and cyclical, taking feedback into account) *and* participative (involving stakeholder views, preparation and participation). Designed particularly for **public sector** and **non-profit organisations**, with multiple stakeholders, the model emphasises a shared-power, political process to develop consensus.

Advantages of rational planning model:

- It provides a structure and impetus for environmental monitoring, data gathering, problem-solving and decision-making
- It encourages a long-term, broad-scope view
- It provides a channel for communicating the corporate vision
- It sets up a control system
- It provides a sense of shared purpose, direction and security

However, some have argued that this is an ideal model which is rare in practice. Decision-making is, in fact, constrained by a number of factors, such as:

- Lack of sufficient, or sufficiently accurate, information
- Lack of time to evaluate all options

- Uncertainty about future conditions
- The need to compromise or negotiate (about ends as well as means)
- The decision-makers' own imperfect perceptions.

Emergent strategy and logical incrementalism

Emergent strategy is the idea that strategy is not always the result of senior management intentions, but may arise out of a series of decisions and actions over time. Strategy is a 'developing pattern in a stream of decisions'.

Quinn argued that there are good reasons why managers may proceed by means of short steps, building on strategies already in place, and making only limited changes. This doesn't necessarily mean just 'muddling through' (or 'disjointed incrementalism'). Quinn advocated a process which he called logical incrementalism: 'the deliberate development of strategy by experimentation and learning from partial commitments rather than through global formulations of total strategies.'

Such an approach:

- Allows the firm to be flexible and opportunistic
- Encourages participation, learning and creativity at all levels
- Avoids the tendency to become obsessed with implementing a chosen or intended strategy, which leads to rigidity in the face of environmental changes
- Avoids the tendency to become complacent about realised strategy

Managing intended and realised strategy

An organisation may well have a formally stated *intended* strategy (as a result of deliberate planning processes) – while, in practice, it is actually pursuing a completely different set of *realised* strategies. Organisational performance may end up disconnected from formal statements of mission, values and objectives – and the expectations of customers, employees and other stakeholders.

Realised strategy may diverge from intended strategy where:

- Intended strategy is deliberately formulated by senior management in the form of plans – but these are not implemented, or are partially or differently implemented in practice
- Realised strategy is partly the outcome of emergent, opportunistic or adaptive strategy processes
- Aspects of the intended strategy are unrealised: that is, they do not come about.

Implications for strategists:

- Managers need to be aware of the problem, and have access to feedback which enables them to check whether intended strategy is being realised in practice.
- Managers need to avoid over-confidence in strategic planning systems.
- Emergent strategy processes need to be managed.

- Managers need to be intentional about monitoring environmental changes, threats and opportunities – and developing strategy to meet them.

Duncan classifies environmental conditions on two dimensions.

- **Static or dynamic**: referring to the extent, significance and pace of change in the environment
- **Simple or complex**: referring to the ease with which environmental conditions, characteristics, dynamics and effects can be understood.

In simple, static conditions, the environment is relatively straightforward, stable and predictable. Long-range formal strategic planning may be feasible, and strategic continuity (relying on past experience and decisions) may be permissible. However, such conditions may make it difficult for an organisation to develop and leverage distinctive sources of competitive advantage, since all players in the market will be responding to the same conditions. This could put the emphasis on price-based competition, resulting in low profitability.

Where conditions are dynamic or turbulent, the priority will be to make sense of an uncertain future – rather than simply extrapolating from the past. Managers will need to:

- Encourage proactive environmental scanning and feedback-seeking at all levels of the organisation
- Utilise scenario planning techniques
- Develop organisation structures and cultures for agility
- Encourage organisational learning
- See strategy development in terms of logical incrementalism or opportunistic strategy.

OWN NOTES

3

OWN NOTES

CHAPTER 4

Strategic Position

The environment of strategic management

A system has been defined as '... a whole that cannot be taken apart without loss of its essential characteristics' or 'an entity which consists of interdependent parts'.

The organisation as an open system

The environment can be seen as a series of concentric circles.

- The **internal environment** of the organisation consists of its formal organisation structure; its style, climate or 'culture'; its systems and technology; its strategic objectives and plans; policies, procedures, rules and informal practices; and so on.
- The immediate operating or **micro environment** of the organisation includes the stakeholders who directly impact on its operations.
- The general or **macro environment** incorporates wider factors in the market and society in which the organisation operates: industry structure, the national and international economy, law, politics, culture, technological development and natural resources – and so on. This is often analysed using the 'STEEPLE' framework.

The external environment influences the organisation in three ways.

- It presents *threats* and *opportunities*.
- It is the source of *resources* needed by the organisation.
- It contains *stakeholders* who may seek, or have the right, to influence the activities of the organisation.

In order for organisations to interact with their environments effectively, they must undertake systematic analysis of environmental factors, influences and trends. Steps involved: audit environmental influences; assess nature of the environment; identify key environmental forces; identify competitive position; identify opportunities and threats.

The macro environment

A popular tool for analysing external macro environment or supply market factors is described by the acronym STEEPLE.

The STEEPLE framework

FACTORS	EXAMPLES
Socio-cultural	Demographics; consumerism; education and skilling infrastructure; values; attitudes to work; cultural differences; gender roles
Technological	ICT developments; automation facilitating workforce rationalisation; automation changing job roles and organisation
Economic	The economic strength and stability of the nation and industry; rates of inflation, interest and taxation; in international supply markets exchange rates, comparative wages and taxes, freedom of labour and capital movements, trade agreements and so on.
Environmental (or 'ecological')	Consumer demand and public pressure for eco-friendly products and processes; law and regulation; emerging and local priorities re green 'issues'; availability, scarcity and price of natural resources and commodities
Political	Government policies; grants and subsidies available; political risk (eg political or civil unrest or war)
Legal	A wide range of law and regulation on issues such as: employment rights and obligations; workplace health and safety; equal opportunity; working hours; minimum wage; environmental protection; competition; consumer rights; contracts; data protection; and public sector procurement.
Ethical	Consumer demand for ethically sourced and produced goods and services; ethical codes and standards; ethical and reputational risk; the 'employer brand' of the organisation.

Having gathered and classified information on critical factors, changes and trends, using the STEEPLE framework, managers can consider the implications for their organisation.

Using a STEEPLE analysis

FACTOR	DESCRIPTION	ANALYSIS
Socio-cultural	Changing composition, attitudes, values, consumption patterns and education of the population	How might changes affect the demands and expectations of customers, suppliers and other stakeholders, or skill availability?
Technological	Changing tools for design and manufacturing, information and communications etc.	Are there opportunities for development – or risks of obsolescence? Are competitors adapting more quickly?
Economic	Growth trends; patterns of employment, income, rates of interest, exchange, tax etc.	How might changes affect future demand for your products or services, or future supply and cost of resources and labour?
Ecological	Resources, sustainability, pollution management, weather, 'green' pressures	Which factors may cause supply or logistical problems, compliance issues, market pressure or risk to reputation?
Political	Government influence on your industry	What are the likely implications of a change in government policy?
Legal	Law and regulation on business, employment, information etc.	How will the organisation need to adapt its policies and practices in order to comply with forthcoming measures?
Ethical	Corporate values, stakeholder pressure and established standards for fair and ethical trading and employment, and corporate governance	What activities or areas of the supply chain may expose the organisation to sustainability, compliance and/or reputational risk?

Industries and sectors

According to Porter, five forces determine the extent of competition in an industry.

- Threats from new entrants
- Threats from substitute products
- Buyers' bargaining power
- Suppliers' bargaining power
- The intensity of rivalry within the industry

Barriers to entry:

- Economies of scale and other cost advantages for established competitors
- High capital investment requirements in order to enter the market
- Product differentiation and brand identity
- Switching costs and customer loyalty to existing brands

- Existing players' control over supply and distribution channels
- Existing players' control over a natural resource
- Restricted labour or skill supply
- Government policy and legislative barriers

Barriers to exit:

- A lack of assets with significant break-up, re-sale or re-use value
- The cost of redundancy payments
- Effects on other divisions or activities
- Reputational damage
- Corporate social responsibility and/or government pressure

Buyers are particularly powerful in the following situations.

- They are limited in number and/or large in size, relative to supplying firms.
- Their spend is a high proportion of suppliers' revenue.
- Products and services are undifferentiated.
- There is potential for 'backward integration'.

Suppliers are particularly powerful in the following situations.

- They are limited in number and/or large in size, relative to buying firms.
- There are few substitute products.
- The volume purchased by the buyer is not important to the supplier.
- The supplier's product is an important component in the buyer's business.
- The switching cost for buyers is high.
- There is potential for 'forward integration'.

Like organisms, many aspects of organisations and industries can be seen as progressing through lifecycle stages of birth, growth, maturity, decline and death. Lifecycle models are used to describe the growth and decline of products and industries, and supplier and customer relationships. The lifecycle stage reached by a product or industry will be an important determinant of competitive behaviour.

- Where the market for a product or service is growing, an organisation may seek to achieve its own growth through growth in the market.
- Once markets are mature, organisational growth can only be achieved at the expense of competitors.
- In markets where product lifecycles are short, there will be a premium on competitive competencies such as market research, innovation, responsiveness, supply chain agility, and supply chain management to support fast idea-to-market cycles.

Competitors and markets

Strategic planners need to identify, understand and target their strategies in relation to:

- Their **direct competitors**
- Their **markets**

It may therefore be helpful for an organisation to identify and analyse the **strategic groups** that represent their most direct, or comparable, competitors. Strategic groups are effectively segments of an industry or sector: organisation types which identifiably share some strategic characteristics and priorities.

The identification of strategic groups may help strategic planners to:

- Identify the **most direct competitors** of the organisation
- Identify the **basis of competition** within the group
- Identify **opportunities and threats** arising from the nature and intensity of competition within the relevant strategic group
- Assess the **potential to enter** another strategic group.

A market consists of both current and potential customers with the ability to buy a product or service. Market segmentation is 'the process of dividing a potential market into distinct subsets of consumers with common needs or characteristics'. Three broad targeting strategies:

- Undifferentiated marketing
- Differentiated marketing
- Concentrated marketing

Market segments must exhibit four characteristics if they are to be useful: measurability; substantiality; accessibility; actionability.

Possible segmentation bases:

- Geographical area
- Demographics
- Psychographics
- Product end use or benefit
- Buyer behaviour and preferences
- Distribution channel

The stakeholder environment

Stakeholders are individuals and groups who have a legitimate interest or 'stake' in an organisation, process, project or decision. They may have invested money in it, or contributed to it, or they may be affected by its activities and outcomes.

- **Internal stakeholders**, eg directors, managers and employees
- **Connected stakeholders**, eg shareholders, financiers, customers, suppliers
- **External stakeholders**, eg government, regulatory bodies, pressure groups, local communities.

The widening of an organisation's responsibilities to less directly connected groups is a major trend in modern business, under the umbrella term of **corporate social responsibility** (CSR). Businesses have, in particular, become increasingly aware of the need to maintain a positive reputation in the marketplace, and this may require a more inclusive approach to stakeholder management, which recognises the legitimate needs and concerns of wider, secondary or 'indirect' stakeholders.

Stakeholder management recognises the need to take stakeholders into account when formulating strategies and plans. For a procurement and supply chain manager, stakeholder management is likely to be helpful in several ways.

- It enables you to gain expert input from stakeholders at the planning stage of a project.
- Stakeholders are more likely to 'own' and support plans to which they have had input.
- Gaining the support of powerful stakeholders may, in turn, mobilise power and resources within the organisation in support of your plans.
- At the very least, sources of resistance to your plans can be anticipated and planned for.

Mendelow's power/interest matrix is the best known specialist tool of stakeholder mapping. It maps stakeholders according to their power to influence purchasing activity and the likelihood of their showing an interest in it.

Mendelow's power/interest matrix

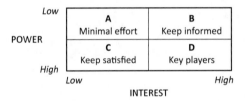

The internal environment

The overarching structure of strategic planning may be expressed as: 'Where are we now?', 'Where do we want to get to?' and 'How will we get from here to there?'

A position audit is a systematic examination of the organisation's **current state**, in order to identify its strengths and weaknesses in areas such as the following.

- Its resources and assets (human, financial, information, physical, reputational etc)
- Its products, brands and markets
- Its operating, administrative, managerial and information systems
- Its internal organisation and structure
- Its distinctive competencies and capabilities
- Its performance and results (using financial and non-financial criteria)

Techniques of internal/position analysis

Resource audit	Assessing the resources that the organisation owns, controls or can access to support its competitive position and strategies. Resources are strategically significant if they are: scarce; vulnerable to supply fluctuations or disruption; critical to the organisation's business or processes; and/or a source of competitive advantage.
Skills audit	Assessing the skills available in the organisation to cope with current and future demands.
Knowledge audit	Assessing the key knowledge or intellectual property that the organisation owns, controls or can access.
Value chain analysis (VCA)	Utilising the value chain model to identify potential for the elimination of wastes and the addition of further value at various points and activities in the value chain.
Supply chain analysis	Mapping participants, flows and linkages in the supply chain, in order to identify sources of waste, inefficiency and cost.
Portfolio analysis	Assessing the current position and future potential of the organisation's portfolio of products and services in different markets or market segments.
Benchmarking	Measuring products, processes and practices against those of competitors, industry leaders or accredited standards.

Competencies are 'the activities or processes through which the organisation deploys its resources effectively'.

- **Threshold** competencies are the basic capabilities necessary to support a particular strategy or to enable the organisation to compete in a given market.
- **Core** competencies are distinctive value-creating skills, capabilities and resources which add value in the eyes of the customer; are scarce and difficult for competitors to imitate; and are flexible for future needs.

Strategic gaps

Corporate appraisal is the term given to 'a critical assessment of the strengths and weaknesses, opportunities and threats in relation to the internal and environmental factors affecting an entity, in order to establish its condition prior to the preparation of the long-term plan'.

Strengths, weaknesses, opportunities and threats (SWOT) analysis is a technique of corporate appraisal, used to assess the **internal** resources of an organisation (or function or project) to cope with and/or capitalise on factors in the **external** environment in which it operates. Data will be fed into this process from external and internal environmental analyses.

Strengths and weaknesses are *internal* aspects of the business that enhance or limit its ability to compete, change and thrive, such as:

- Physical and financial resources
- The product portfolio, and its competitive strength
- Human resources
- The efficiency and effectiveness of functions and operations
- The efficiency and effectiveness of systems
- Organisation structure
- Distinctive competencies

Opportunities and threats are factors in the *external* environment that may emerge to impact on the business. What potential do they offer to either enhance or erode its competitive advantage or profitability?

The term 'strategic gap' describes 'an opportunity in the competitive environment that is not being fully exploited by competitors.'

- STEEPLE analysis may identify threats and opportunities presented by macro-environmental factors.
- Five Forces analysis may identify threats such as falling barriers to entry, the emergence of substitute products or a rise in buyer or supplier power.
- Strategic group analysis may identify market gaps, with opportunities to enter a different strategic group.
- Market segmentation may identify opportunities such as the potential to leverage specialist expertise to service a 'niche' market.

OWN NOTES

OWN NOTES

CHAPTER 5

Competitive Strategy

Value and added value strategies

Porter: an organisation's competitive advantage ultimately comes from the 'value' it creates for its customers.

- An organisation creates value – by performing its activities more effectively or efficiently than its competitors *and*
- Customers purchase value – by comparing an organisation's products and services with those of its competitors.

Organisations can add value through enhancing product quality or design; value for money; delivery and availability; brand appeal; exclusivity; service levels; and so on.

The main focus for procurement and supply chain management is arguably value added either by **cutting costs** (without loss of quality or product features) *or* by **securing operational efficiency** (enabling superior quality or features at no additional cost). Ideally, it might aim to achieve both of these objectives: improved output at reduced cost.

Porter's value chain

The individual firm's value chain does not exist in isolation, and value-adding activities do not stop at the organisation's boundaries. Competitive advantage can be achieved anywhere along the internal business value chain – but a firm must also secure competitive advantage by managing the *linkages within its supply network:* the basis of techniques such as lean and agile supply, total quality management and supply chain management. This wider value chain, extended through the supply chain, is known as a **value system** or **value network**.

It is important to consider value from the point of view of strategic customers, as the basis for value creation and the development of strategic capability. It is also important to remember that different groups of customers may value different characteristics or benefits of a product or service, and that this will affect the bases on which organisations compete.

- **Threshold** product and service features are standard features which customers would expect from any provider in the market or market segment
- **Critical success factors (CSFs)** are features which are seen as particularly important by customers, and on the basis of which one provider in a market or market segment may be preferred over another.

Generic competitive strategies

Porter suggested that a firm may seek two basic kinds of competitive advantage, or 'edge' over its rivals in a market: low cost or differentiation. In other words, competitive advantage is obtained *either* by:

- Providing comparable value to the customer more efficiently than competitors (low cost), *or* by
- Performing activities at comparable cost but in unique or distinctive ways, creating more value for customers than competitors and commanding a premium price (differentiation).

At the same time, an organisation can choose to apply either of these strategies *either* to a broad market *or* to a narrow-focused or targeted market (or market segment).

For organisations competing in a price-sensitive market, cost leadership is the key strategic imperative. Such organisations need a thorough understanding of their costs and cost drivers, and of their customers' definition of quality. Their essential task is then to supply acceptable quality at the lowest possible unit cost: specifically, at a low cost level relative to competitors.

Pursuing an overall cost leadership strategy will require an SBU to adopt tactics such as: large-scale production for economies of scale ('high-volume, low-cost'); enhancing productivity through technology; seeking continual improvement and waste reduction; and minimising overhead and supply costs. In high-technology and highly skilled industries, producing more items than competitors may also allow the firm to benefit from the learning or experience curve effect, to achieve lower average costs.

From a procurement and supply chain perspective, the major implication of a cost leadership strategy is the emphasis on cost reduction, through measures such as inventory minimisation, robust requirements and transport planning, variety reduction and quality control, transaction streamlining, price negotiation, aggregation of requirements, supply base rationalisation and so on.

Developing an offering that is perceived to be unique in the market is an obvious defensive response for an organisation faced by a strong low-cost competitor. Differentiation creates customer and brand loyalty, which is a barrier to entry to new competitors and reduces the firm's vulnerability to other competitive pressures such as substitutes, buyer power (since it is less easy to switch) and supplier power (since high margins can offset cost increases).

From a supply chain perspective, a differentiation strategy permits, encourages – and arguably, requires – closer collaborative relationships with suppliers. Supply chain expertise and effectiveness can contribute to a wide range of differentiation variables. Process and product improvement will be key aims, along with quality control, and support for innovation.

Innovation capability and leadership supports differentiation through: technology leverage; excellent product functionality and design; unique product features; continually 'new', adapting and improving features; and a loyal brand following among early adopters and style leaders.

An organisation may target its offerings to a particular buyer group, market segment or geographical region. A focus strategy 'targets a narrow segment or domain of activity and tailors its products or services to the needs of that specific segment to the exclusion of others'.

- Cost focus seeks cost leadership within a target market. Cost focusers 'identify areas where broader cost-based strategies fail because of the added costs of trying to satisfy a wide range of needs'.
- Differentiation focus (or 'niche' strategy) develops an offering targeted to appeal to a particular market segment. Differentiation focusers 'look for specific needs that broader differentiators do not serve so well'.

The strategy clock

The strategy clock offers a different way of considering generic competitive strategies. Rather than creating 'either/or' choices between cost-leadership and differentiation strategies, its more dynamic 'circular' view allows for more nuanced strategies, and for incremental adjustments which shift strategy over time. It is also an explicitly marketing-oriented model, focusing on key aspects of the customer value proposition: product benefits (as perceived by the customer) and price (to the customer, rather than cost to the producer).

The strategy clock

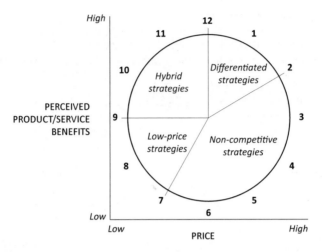

Non-competitive strategies occupy a zone in which the economics are un-feasible or un-sustainable: customers are being asked to pay prices which are too high for the perceived benefits, representing poor value for money. Such strategies are likely to lead to failure.

Low-price strategies are feasible strategies allowing for building on positive customer perceptions of price and value. In this model, there is a range of strategies available.

- Close to the 9 o'clock point, a *low-price* strategy (representing reasonable benefits and value compared to competitors) would be aimed at market penetration, or gaining market share.
- Alternatively, the company may be able to offer lower benefits for a low price (nearer 7 o'clock), appealing to customers on the basis of a *no frills* budget-product strategy.

Differentiation strategies are feasible strategies for building on positive customer perceptions of the benefits offered by the product or service.

- Close to the 12 o'clock point, a strategy of *differentiation* (high perceived benefits) at relatively moderate prices (ie *without price premium*) would be aimed at market penetration, or gaining market share.
- Again, if the high benefits are costly, this may not be sustainable, and once the product has become established, the company might shift towards a 2 o'clock position: *differentiation with price premium*.
- 2 o'clock represents a point at which benefits are reduced while prices are increased: this may only be sustainable in selected market segments and would represent a *differentiation focus* strategy in Porter's terms.

Sustaining competitive advantage

Competitive advantage based on low prices might be sustainable in the long term if:

- The company is prepared to accept reduced profit margins
- The company is prepared to risk a price war
- The company has distinctive strategic competencies
- The company is prepared to focus on market segments which are particularly price sensitive.

Competitive advantage based on differentiation might be sustainable if:

- The basis of differentiation is difficult for competitors to imitate
- There are high switching costs in the market
- The company's cost position provides relatively high profit margins

Two views of competitive strategy:

- A **positioning-based approach** to strategy suggests that the source of an organisation's competitive advantage lies mainly in how it achieves strategic 'fit' with its external environment, exploiting opportunities and minimising threats. In other words, you set your strategic objectives by identifying product or market opportunities within a given environment, and then develop and deploy the organisational resources required to get you to where you want to be.
- The **resource-based approach** suggests that the source of an organisation's competitive advantage lies mainly in how it exploits its distinctive internal resources and competencies, setting strategic objectives based on what they enable it to do. In this 'inside-out' approach, you start with the organisation's strengths, and seek an environment that will enable you to exploit them: the organisation will change environments to suit what it does best – rather than changing what it does best to fit the environment.

Porter's generic competitive strategies are essentially based on a positioning approach. But some argue that competitive advantage based on positioning is not sustainable in the long term.

Not all organisational resources are a potential source of competitive advantage. In order to be advantage-creating, resources must be:

- Valuable: capable of creating customer (and shareholder) value
- Rare and in high demand
- Inimitable or difficult for competitors to imitate
- Difficult to substitute.

Competencies are 'the activities or processes through which the organisation deploys its resources effectively'. 'Senior managers must conceive of their companies as a portfolio of core competencies, rather than just a portfolio of businesses and products' – and the same could be argued of supply chains.

Andrew Cox's relational competence model suggests that the greater a buyer's reliance on suppliers to secure strategic competencies, the greater the depth of the supply relationship will need to be. Core competencies should be retained within the firm, or controlled through merger or acquisition.

Competition and collaboration

'Advantage may not always be achieved by competition alone. Collaboration between organisations may be a crucial ingredient in achieving advantage – or avoiding competition. Also, organisations simultaneously may compete in some markets and collaborate in others.'

In general strategic terms, competitiveness might actively be improved by network collaboration, where its effects are to enhance the elements of the Five Forces framework in the organisation's favour. Collaborative strategies may embrace other organisations and constituencies including suppliers and distributors (in supply networks); competitors (eg in buying consortia or multi-stakeholder industry groups); customers (eg in co-opting customers to define value, or to engage in 'co-production' through self-service options); and other stakeholders.

Game theory is a branch of applied mathematics and economics. The theory studies situations where players make decisions in an attempt to maximise their returns. As applied to strategic management, game theory seeks to explain the complex dynamics of competition and collaboration among a set of competitors or 'players' in a market.

Implications of game theory:

- In some cases, collaboration can lead to a better joint outcome.
- Co-operation will be difficult in a market where there is lack of transparency about the bases of competition.
- Co-operation is more likely where there are few competitors in the market.
- The outcomes may be improved by an organisation's 'playing' with the same supplier or customer repeatedly over the long term, favouring co-operation or accommodation of both parties' best interests.

At one end of the relationship spectrum there are **competitive** relationships, in which buyer and supplier compete for share of value. This is traditionally associated with transactional or arm's length procurements, and adversarial relations.

Shortcomings of the traditional adversarial model.

- The emphasis on confrontation, rather than co-operation, means that each party fails to derive the full benefits of the other party's expertise (let alone potential synergies).
- Time and management effort are wasted because each purchase is in principle a new negotiation, rather than building on relational foundations.
- More waste arises from the size of the supply base, each supplier requiring identification, screening, evaluation, motivation, management and so on.
- Suppliers are unlikely to be focused or motivated by small, short-term contracts: effort

will have to go into performance management in order to secure compliance with standards (let alone proactive improvement or super-performance).

- There is little potential for improved quality and reduced costs arising from integration and co-operation (eg just in time supply, early supplier involvement and so on).

At the other end of the spectrum, therefore, there are **collaborative** relationships, in which buying and supplying organisations work together (more or less closely) for mutual benefit. At the high-trust, high-integration end of the spectrum are outsourcing relationships, strategic alliances, partnership relations and co-destiny relationships.

Co-operative relationships take time and effort to develop. They are not possible with all suppliers – and may not be cost-effective for routine items. They may also miss out unnecessarily on the opportunity to appropriate a larger value share. And there are risks and obstacles inherent in co-operative supply chain management.

Supply chain strategies

Potential contributions of highly motivated suppliers:

- New product development and process innovation
- Availability and delivery
- Quality
- Value for money
- Service, advice and information

In more general terms, however, positive supplier relationship management can itself offer a range of benefits for an organisation.

- Stronger relationships
- Sound risk management
- Better return on relationship investment
- Improved business efficiency
- Greater profitability
- Potential for value-adding synergy
- Improved corporate social responsibility and reputation management
- Competitive advantage

Examples of strategic relationship management models:

- Supplier relationship management (SRM)
- Customer relationship management (CRM)
- Vendor managed inventory (VMI)
- Collaborative planning, forecasting and replenishment (CPFR)
- Partnership sourcing
- Supplier development.

Strategic cost reduction measures:

- Restructuring
- Centralising purchasing or decentralising purchasing
- Process engineering or re-engineering
- Developing collaborative strategic relationships for cost and price advantages
- Applying ICT and automation technologies
- Rationalising the suplier base
- Developing 'lean' supply and production
- Collaborating with key supply chain partners on cost reduction programmes
- Investigating the potential for global and low-cost country sourcing
- Considering the outsourcing (or offshoring) of non-core activities

Effective supply chain management can support the management and reduction of costs.

- Collaboration on cost reduction programmes
- Increasing the visibility of supply chain processes, enabling areas of waste to be identified
- Supporting the optimising of end-to-end supply chain costs
- Supporting better information sharing, activity co-ordination and collaborative planning
- Supporting proactive quality assurance and management
- Encouraging buyer-side and supplier-side systems integration
- Creating long-term, stable and mutually beneficial commercial relationships
- Supporting whole-life contracts

The supply chain has a crucial role in maintaining and assuring quality.

- At a strategic level, this may involve supplier relationship management, early supplier involvement, supplier selection and development policies, quality management and continuous improvement strategies, supplier accreditation and development and the establishment of systems for controlling supplier performance.
- At the operational level, it includes matters such as materials specification, service level agreements, contracting, supplier evaluation, quality control, benchmarking, contract management and so on.

Effective supply chain management can support reduced time-to-market product development (idea-to-market) cycles by:

- Creating a pool of trusted expert suppliers, and a collaborative approach
- Encouraging end-to-end proactive management of supply chain processes
- Encouraging demand chain management and data-sharing
- Developing supply chain 'agility' or responsiveness

Effective supply chain management can also support reduced order cycle and delivery times.

'Lean production is "lean" because it uses less of every thing compared with mass production: half the human effort in the factory, half the factory space, half the investment in tools, half the engineering hours to develop a new product in half the time. Also, it requires far less than half of the needed inventory on site. The expected results are fewer defects, while producing a greater and ever growing variety of products'.

Lean supply is: 'the elimination of duplication of effort and capability in the supply chain, combined with a philosophy of continuously increasing the expectations of performance and self-imposed pressure to excel.' Lean supply networks collaborate intentionally, in order to progressively eliminate cost and waste (at any and all points of the supply chain), with the overall goal of optimising the customer value stream.

Agile supply is 'using market knowledge and a responsive supply network to exploit profitable opportunities in the marketplace'. An agile organisation, for example, is better able to exploit opportunities for product modification at any time that the market appears ready for it.

- Lean philosophy is most powerful when the winning criteria are cost and quality
- Agility is paramount where service and customer value enhancement are key.

Effective supply chain management supports **innovation** through:

- Enhanced access to market intelligence
- Faster and more effective product design and development processes
- Tapping into synergies and opportunities available from pooling information, ideas and expertise within the supply network
- Creating incentives for supply chain partners to innovate
- The intentional selection of long-term strategic supply chain partners with competitive competencies, with innovation capability or potential as a key qualification criterion
- Supporting the use of collaborative techniques
- Supporting the ongoing development of supplier innovation capability
- Supporting supply chain management techniques which are themselves regarded as 'innovative'
- Supporting continuous supply chain improvement and development

A supply chain management approach, built on effective long-term, collaborative partnerships with trusted suppliers, is explicitly recommended as a sourcing strategy for procurements representing a high degree of **supply risk** for the buying organisation.

5

OWN NOTES

CHAPTER 6

Directional and International Strategy

Directional strategies

Ansoff's matrix:

The Ansoff matrix (marketing)			Adapted for wider strategic choice		

	Existing product	New product		Existing product	New product
New market	Market development	Diversification	*New market*	Market development New segments New territories New uses	Diversification On existing competencies With new competencies
Existing market	Market penetration	Product development	*Existing market*	Market penetration Withdrawal Consolidation Market penetration	Product development On existing competencies With new competencies

Directional strategies will not always be strategies of growth – three strategies for existing products in existing markets: withdrawal; consolidation; market penetration.

A strategy of **product development** involves introducing new (or modified or complementary) products to existing markets. Some form of product development will be necessary for long-term survival in fast-changing markets.

A strategy of **market development** concentrates on finding new markets for existing products. An organisation might consider this strategy if it is restricted in its current markets: perhaps they are nearing saturation, or the product is becoming obsolete.

In general strategy terms, the term '**diversification**' covers any strategy aimed at increasing organisational scope by widening the range of products or markets served by the organisation. Within the Ansoff matrix, a strategy of diversification refers more specifically to the development of new products for new markets: effectively, widening the range of products or markets served by the organisation.

Diversification is generally considered the most high-risk strategy, as the organisation faces an initial learning curve with both the product and the market. In order to minimise the risk, the firm may seek to enter new product markets within the same industry or with other relationships to the existing business (**related diversification**), in order to build on the assets or activities it has already developed, or they may acquire (or partner with) other companies already in the market. Alternatively, a firm may embark on **unrelated diversification**: diversifying into products and markets with no relationships to the existing business.

Portfolio matrices

Portfolio matrices are a range of tools and models which can be used by corporate strategic managers to make decisions about strategic investment priorities within and across their business portfolio: that is, about which SBUs to invest in.

Four major strategies are often identified in regard to SBUs and portfolio segments.

- Build: invest (forgoing short-term earnings and profits) to increase future market share
- Hold: consolidate and maintain the current position
- Harvest: reap short-term earnings and profits
- Divest: withdraw to release resources for use elsewhere.

The BCG growth/share matrix:

- **Stars** are business units (or products) with a high market share in a growing market.
- **Question marks** (or problem children) are business units (or products) which have an as yet relatively low market share in a growth market.
- **Cash cows** are business units (or products) which have a high market share in a mature (low-growth) market.
- **Dogs** are business units (or products) which have a low share of a static or declining market.

The General Electric/McKinsey & Co directional policy matrix (or 'business screen') categorises SBUs according to their 'prospects', based on two dimensions.

- The **attractiveness of the market** in which they are operating, in terms of growth potential (eg using STEEPLE or five forces analysis)
- The competitive **strength of the business** in the market (eg using competitor analysis)

This matrix is valuable in adding nuance and being less prescriptive, compared to the simpler BCG model.

The term 'corporate parent' is used to refer to the corporate-level or 'head office' strategic planning unit which sets strategic direction for the SBUs that make up the organisational business portfolio.

The parenting matrix argues that a business should only be included in the corporate portfolio (acquired or retained) if – in addition to reasonable prospects – there is a 'fit' with the strategic capabilities of the parent company: that is, if the activities, decisions and resources of the parent company are likely to **add value to the SBU**.

Where there is no added value (eg because the SBU performs more effectively without association with, or direction or 'interference' from, the corporate parent), the corporate parent may be costing the SBU more than it is contributing: recommended course is to divest or de-couple the SBU from the corporate portfolio.

The parenting matrix maps businesses on two dimensions.

- **Feel**: the fit between the SBU's critical success factors (CSFs) and the corporate parent's capabilities and characteristics.
- **Benefit**: the fit between the SBU's parenting needs or opportunities (areas where parenting could add value to the business), and the capabilities of the corporate parent.

Drivers of internationalisation

Globalisation is 'the increasing integration of internationally dispersed economic activities'.

This integration may involve the globalisation of **markets**, **production** and **finance**.

George S Yip suggested that four groups of factors form the main drivers for any given industry to become globalised: market factors; cost factors; government factors; competition factors.

- Market
- Cost
- Government
- Competition

There are two main sources of advantage available through international strategy.

- The exploitation of **locational advantages**, in the form of the distinctive infrastructure, resource and capability strengths of the organisation's 'home' region or country of operation, which can be leveraged in an international market
- The development of an **international value network**, whereby the distinctive infrastructure, resource and capability strengths of *other* countries and regions can be exploited 'in order to locate each element of the value chain in that country or region where it can be conducted most effectively and efficiently.'

'Porter's Diamond' suggests that locational advantages arise from:

- Local factor conditions
- Local demand conditions
- Local related and supporting industries
- Local firm strategy, industry structure and competitive rivalry

In addition to underpinning *domestic* advantages, organisations may seek advantage from the way in which their international value network is configured: seeking to maximise advantage from the distinctive resources and strengths of different countries and regions. Locational advantages in different overseas product and supply markets may include:

- **Cost advantages:** eg lower labour costs, lower logistics and transportation costs, or economic incentives (tax breaks, investment incentives and so on)
- **Local resources and competencies:** eg the availability of special expertise, academic, research or innovation bodies and so on
- **National or regional market characteristics**, creating market segments and 'niches' for differentiated product offerings.

Dimensions of internationalisation strategy

The global-local dilemma:

- **Globalisation** (or standardisation) means that a company operating in international markets provides the same offering and branding worldwide.
- **Adaptation** means that the company changes its product and marketing mix to suit local needs and conditions.

Standardisation has many advantages.

- Economies of scale in production
- Economies of scale in research and development and new product development
- Economies in marketing
- Potential for consumer retention and loyalty, given a globally mobile customer base
- Promotional, branding and reputational benefits
- Exploitation of the general standardisation of business-to-business market requirements.

Adaptation allows more competitive targeting of products and promotions to local market demands, giving them greater relevance, value – and perhaps quality – in local market conditions.

In practice, organisations often seek to find a balance of local responsiveness with the benefits of global scale: 'thinking global, acting local'.

Porter provides a helpful matrix to show four basic generic international strategies.

Porter's four international strategies

| | | CONFIGURATION OF ACTIVITIES | |
		Dispersed	Concentrated
COORDINATION OF ACTIVITIES	High	Global	Complex export
	Low	Multi-domestic	Simple export

Market entry strategies:

- **Indirect export** means that a company will sell goods to an intermediary in its home market (domestic trade), and that intermediary will resell the goods abroad.
- **Direct export** means that a company will sell goods directly to an overseas customer or intermediary – and will therefore be involved in international trade.
- **Direct investment** represents a high resource commitment, in which the producer invests in a physical presence in the overseas market.

Global supply chain strategies

Strictly speaking, global sourcing is not the same as international procurement. International procurement is about buying from abroad, or importing.

- Local sourcing implies using suppliers who are 'based within easy reach of the buyer', whether geographically or by other measures of accessibility.
- International sourcing implies the sourcing of goods and services from 'overseas' or other-country suppliers: essentially, 'importing'.
- The term 'global sourcing' has a more strategic flavour, involving the development of an international supply network, from which the company's sourcing requirements can be met flexibly, competitively and in a co-ordinated way.

Increasing integration of global sourcing strategies:

- **Stage 1**: a head-office purchasing department buys items internationally.
- **Stage 2**: the head-office purchasing department seeks the help of overseas SBUs to source items.
- **Stage 3**: international purchasing offices are set up in overseas SBUs.
- **Stage 4**: product design and development, as well as sourcing, are decentralised to overseas sourcing and support teams.
- **Stage 5**: the network of offices is co-ordinated to produce an integrated global sourcing strategy.

Benefits of international sourcing:

- Access to required materials, facilities and/or skills
- Availability of culturally distinctive goods
- Access to a wider supplier base
- Opportunities for cost savings
- Exchange rate advantages
- Competitive quality
- Reduced regulatory and compliance burden
- Leveraging available ICT developments for virtual organisation etc
- Support for supply chain agility
- Ability to compete with competitors who are benefiting from any or all of the above advantages.

Drivers for the increase in international and global sourcing:

- Improvements in transport technology
- Improvements in ICT
- Progressive reductions in trade barriers
- Sourcing efficiencies
- Country or region-specific supply factors
- Harmonisation of technical standards

Risks and challenges of international or global sourcing:

- Socio-cultural differences
- Language barriers
- Legal issues
- Logistical and supply risks
- Exchange rate risk
- Payment risk
- Difficulties of monitoring and assuring quality, environmental and ethical standards in overseas supplier operations
- General STEEPLE factor risks in the overseas environment
- Additional sourcing costs

Low cost countries may be price-competitive because of:

- Cheap skilled labour costs
- Abundance of raw materials and resources
- Low development and production costs
- Currency value and exchange rates
- Favourable taxation regimes
- Lack of bargaining power in the market and supply relationships

It should be obvious that some of these factors pose sustainability issues and risks, with the potential for exploitation of vulnerable suppliers and workers. Some low-cost, developing countries pose significant business, supply and sustainability or reputational risks to buying organisations, and may *not* be an appropriate target for low-cost country sourcing.

OWN NOTES

OWN NOTES

CHAPTER 7

Strategy Methods and Evaluation

Organic development

Advantages of organic development:

- Using existing capabilities to pursue new strategies requires development and experimentation activities, which can drive improved knowledge management, learning and innovation
- Spreading investment over the whole development lifecycle
- Allowing proactive development, independent of availability constraints
- Allowing strategic independence, without the compromises and constraints imposed by mergers or alliances

Merger and acquisition

Mergers and acquisitions:

- A **merger** is where two companies voluntarily pool the ownership interests of their respective shareholders, combining two entities into one (typically as more or less equal partners).
- An **acquisition** (or **takeover) i**s where one firm buys the equity stake or assets of another company.

Both options result in the assets (including the human resources) of two organisations being integrated and jointly managed.

Advantages of mergers and acquisitions:

- Taking advantage of economies of scale and scope
- Giving immediate access to resources
- Giving a high degree of control

7

Motives for M & A

Strategic motives	Extension Consolidation Capability
Financial motives	Financial efficiency Tax efficiency Unbundling
Managerial motives	Personal ambition Bandwagon effects

M & A processes: target choice; target valuation; integration.

Implications of M & A for supply chain strategy

- Potential to access the target firm's developed supply chain network
- The need to integrate and optimise both firms' existing supply chain networks, technologies and systems
- The potential for mutual learning
- The need to leverage increased market power
- The potential for the organisation to reposition itself in the supply chain

Strategic alliance

Benefits of strategic alliance

- Access to the other party's overseas resources and capabilities
- Bringing together complementary capabilities and strengths
- Reduction in the effects of competition
- Economies of scale in joint activities
- Sharing the financial and operational risk of new ventures

Structures for strategic collaboration

- **Joint venture**: a formal arrangement whereby two independent companies establish a new company which they jointly own and manage: a form of **equity alliance**.
- **Strategic alliance:** a formally structured relationship, in which two companies legally contract to cooperate in limited, specified ways: a form of **non-equity alliance**.
- **Subcontracting, outsourcing, franchising and licensing agreements**: non-equity arrangements by which one organisation delegates some of its own activities, under contract, to external companies.
- **Networks**: looser, dynamic, more informal affiliations of autonomous and broadly equal organisations.

Characteristics of partnership sourcing:

- Top-level management commitment
- Involvement by all the relevant disciplines and functions

- Customer and supplier working together
- A high level of trust, knowledge sharing and openness
- Clear joint objectives
- Commitment to a long-term relationship
- A proactive approach to improving and developing the partnership
- A total quality management philosophy
- Flexibility, as a result of enhanced trust and communication
- A high degree of systems integration (eg using EDI)

Which approach?

Four factors in the decision between merger and alliance:

- Urgency
- Uncertainty
- Type of capabilities desired
- Modularity of capabilities desired

Securing strategic capability

Make-or-buy decisions face all organisations, at three levels of planning.

- **Strategic make/do or buy decisions** determine the long-term activities, capabilities, resources and 'boundaries' of the firm.
- **Tactical make-do or buy decisions** reflect the organisation's response to short-term or cyclical changes in demand for its products or services.
- **Operational or 'component' make-or-buy decisions** are basically product design and manufacturing decisions.

Outsourcing is the process whereby an organisation delegates major non-core activities or functions, under contract, to specialist external service providers, potentially on a long-term relational basis. Outsourcing is thus the ultimate expression of a buyer's attitude to the supply chain as an extension of in-house resources, as seen in the concept of supply chain management.

Competencies and contractor competence

| | | COMPETENCE OF CONTRACTORS | |
		High	Low
CORE IMPORTANCE	Low	Outsource/buy in	Develop contracting
	High	Collaboration	In-house

The contribution of a strategic supply chain management approach:

- Encouraging decision-making at a strategic level
- Supporting the use of the value stream or value system
- Forcing managers to take a broad view of the entire supply chain
- Developing supply chain relationships to support decision-making

Value chain (re-)positioning: The concept of **repositioning** an organisation within the supply chain or value chain implies the extension of its operations or control to a wider range of upstream or downstream activities – and a greater share of responsibility for creating and adding value. Repositioning may help an organisation to extend its core competencies and capacity, which may offer synergies and suggest other strategic directions.

Strategy evaluation

Key criteria in strategy evaluation:

- **Suitability**. Does the strategy fit the situation identified in the strategic appraisal? Does it address the key opportunities and constraints faced by the organisation?
- **Acceptability**. Does the proposed strategy meet the expectations of stakeholders? Are the levels of risk and likely return acceptable? Will stakeholders accept the strategy?
- **Feasibility**. Can the strategy be implemented? Will it work in practice? Can it be financed? Are people and skill resources available? Can the required resources and capabilities be obtained and integrated?

Suitability:

- Does it capitalise on the organisation's identified strengths and exploit its core competencies (for competitive advantage)?
- Does it overcome identified weaknesses?
- Does it deflect or neutralise identified threats?
- Does it exploit identified opportunities?
- Does it align with the organisation's mission, objectives and cultural values?

Acceptability:

- Will the strategy be sufficiently profitable to meet shareholder expectations?
- Will managers and employees favour the decision?
- What will be the impact on customer satisfaction, loyalty and demand?
- What will be the impact on long-term supply chain relationships?
- What will be the 'external' costs and impacts on the wider community?

Three aspects of acceptability: risk; returns; reactions.

Feasibility:

- Is it practical: do we have the resources?
- Economic (or financial): are the financial resources available?
- Social: will stakeholders accept and support the strategy – or resist it?
- Technical: can the strategy be implemented using available or accessible technology.

Sustainability has also become an extremely important aspect of procurement policy in both the public and private sectors in recent years. The term 'sustainability' describes strategies designed to balance economic viability with considerations of environmental and social responsibility (Profit, Planet and People – sometimes also referred to as the 'Triple Bottom Line').

- Economic sustainability (Profit)
- Environmental sustainability (Planet)
- Social sustainability (People)

7

OWN NOTES

CHAPTER 8

Strategy and Structure

Organisational structure

Objectives of formal organisation structure or design:

- Define work roles and relationships
- Define work tasks and responsibilities
- Channel information flows efficiently through the organisation
- Coordinate goals and activities of different units
- Control the flow of work, information and resources
- Support flexible working and adaptability to changing internal and external demands
- Facilitate organisational learning
- Encourage and support the commitment, involvement and satisfaction of the people who work for the organisation
- Support and improve efficiency and effectiveness

The structure of an organisation should ideally be designed to **support its strategic objectives**, rather than the other way around. However, structure can't always follow strategy in such a straightforward way.

- Structure is influenced and constrained by many factors besides strategic intent.
- Organisations don't always have the luxury of 'designing' a structure from scratch.
- When the environment in which organisations operate is subject to constant change, it is not possible to make radical, frequent structural alterations to match.

Strategy may *partly* follow structure, because the structure is a major factor in the kinds of processes the organisation will be good at, and the kinds of opportunities it will be well-placed to exploit.

A 'good' organisation structure will have (all other factors permitting): clear paths of reporting and accountability; effective mechanisms for multi-directional information flow and co-ordination; efficiently short chains of decision-making; minimal duplication of effort; soft 'vertical' barriers between functions; in-built flexibility. It will be adapted to external and internal constraints (such as corporate governance requirements, or the availability of managerial talent) and will reflect the corporate mission and market strategy.

Signs that a structure may be **ineffective**:

- Slow decision and response times
- Inter-departmental conflicts

- Excessive layers of management
- Lack of co-ordination between units
- High labour turnover among skilled junior staff
- Lack of identifiable accountabilities for key tasks

There are many influences on organisation structure: how far power and authority are centralised; the span of control; the division of labour; the grouping of people into working units; the need for communication channels, and so on.

Structural types

Mintzberg's building blocks of organisational structure:

- The strategic apex
- The operating core
- The middle line
- The technostructure
- Staff support

Mintzberg's five types of organisational structure:

- Simple (or entrepreneurial) structure
- Machine structure (or bureaucracy)
- Professional bureaucracy
- Divisional (independent) structure
- Ad hoc (flexible) structure

In a functional structure tasks are grouped together according to the common nature or focus of the task, and the specialised skills, resources or technology required. Functional structures are well suited to small or start-up organisations, and larger organisations with relatively limited product portfolios.

Here are some alternative methods of organisation.

- Geographical structure
- Product, brand or customer structure

The essence of **matrix structure** is dual authority. Staff in different functions or regions are responsible both:

- to their departmental managers, in regard to the activities of the department; and
- to a product, project or account manager, in regard to the activities of the department related to the given product, project or account.

A **divisional structure** may be the logical extension of these methods of organisation, as units become large enough to support their own managerial overheads, and therefore to become more or less autonomous. Divisionalisation is the division of the organisation into more or less autonomous strategic business units, as the business diversifies into new areas. Divisions may be: profit or investment centres within a company; or subsidiary companies grouped under a holding company.

Three structural options for multi-national organisations:

- **International divisions** may be added alongside a more comprehensive and complex structure of domestic divisions (based on product, brand or region).
- **Local subsidiaries** reflect a geographical divisional structure, having most of the core functions required to operate in a semi-autonomous way within their local market.
- **Global production divisions** may be developed to maximise cost efficiency.

A more radical **transnational structure** may be developed to exploit the advantages of local subsidiary structure (for local responsiveness) *and* global product divisional structure (for economies of scale and co-ordination). Transnational structures have a distinctive focus on: knowledge sharing; specialisation; network management.

Modern trends in organisation aim to create flexible or adaptive structures, which can respond swiftly (and without trauma) to environmental and strategic change. These include: flattening of organisational hierarchies; chunked structures; project management structures; horizontal structures; core-periphery models; network structures; boundaryless structures.

A special form of the network concept is the **virtual organisation**, where companies (or units of a single company) collaborate, coordinate their activities and share data, using information communications technology (ICT) as their main – or only – point of contact.

Structuring supply chain management

Key factors influencing the design of the supply chain management function:

- The size, nature and role of the procurement and supply task
- Subdivision of procurement accountabilities
- Structure and environment in which the function operates

One of the key trends in procurement organisation in recent decades has been the increasing integration of materials-related activities within a single management framework, in response to more holistic views of the supply chain.

An important organisational issue is the extent to which procurement and supply chain responsibilities should be centralised or departmentalised (ie placed in the hands of a single department reporting to a single executive) or decentralised (ie devolved to procurement officers in different SBUs or user departments).

Advantages of centralised purchasing:

- Specialisation of procurement staff
- Potential for the consolidation of requirements
- Greater co-ordination of procurement activities
- Greater standardisation of specifications
- More effective control of procurement activity
- Avoidance of conflict between business divisions
- Access to specialist skills, contacts and resources

Advantages of decentralised purchasing:

- Better communication and coordination between procurement and operating departments
- Customer focus
- Quicker response to operational and user needs and environmental changes and problems
- Knowledge of, and relationships with, locally based suppliers
- Smaller purchase quantities: sacrificing economies of scale, but reducing costs and risks of holding inventory
- Accountability
- Freeing central procurement units to focus on higher-level tasks.

Centralised procurement: a **shared service** approach. A shared service unit (SSU) is a dedicated provider of services to internal users. The SSU is responsible for managing the costs, quality and timeliness of its services.

Hybrid structures: CLAN; SCAN; lead buyer; business partner.

Benefits of **outsourcing procurement**:

- The freeing up of resources
- The ability to draw on specialist procurement knowledge and expertise
- The potential for third-party purchasers to aggregate demand and consolidate orders
- The re-focusing of remaining internal procurement staff on strategic issues
- Greater flexibility to adjust to peaks and troughs of demand

A **buying consortium** is a group of separate organisations that combine together for the purpose of procuring goods or services. Benefits:

- Discounts
- Framework agreements, simplifying purchase administration for members.
- Pooling of expertise, knowledge and contacts

Cross-functional teams and project work

Drivers of cross-functional teamworking in procurement:

- The increasing involvement of procurement staff in strategic decisions
- The increasing adoption of a supply chain philosophy
- Its ability to make best use of developments in ICT
- The adoption of advanced world class systems
- The increasing complexity and dynamism of global markets and technologies
- The need to leverage human resource capability

Difficulties:

- Added potential for time-consuming complexity, conflict and consensus-seeking.
- Lack of clear lines of authority
- All teams take time to develop

- Difficulties of dual authority structures
- Practical difficulties of organising meetings and information flows

Structuring the supply chain

An organisation might adopt a deliberate policy of tiering its suppliers, so as to reduce the number of first-tier suppliers: the 'vendor/supplier base' with which it has to deal directly. This may be part of a process of supplier rationalisation or supply chain re-structuring, for example. The organisation deals directly only with its first-tier suppliers: second-tier suppliers deal with a first-tier supplier.

Implications for supply chain management:

- The sourcing, selection and contracting of the first-tier suppliers will be a crucial strategic exercise.
- There will be fewer commercial relationships to manage.
- The top-tier organisation will still need to 'drill down' through the tiers in the supply chain
- The buyer may exercise influence over the first-tier supplier to adopt some of its own existing suppliers as subcontractors or lower-tier suppliers.
- More and better supply chain improvements and innovations.
- Procurement may be freed up to pursue a more strategic focus.

Management issues in closed-loop supply chains:

- Effective supply base management, integration and collaboration
- Effective supplier and customer relationships
- Supplier selection and contract award on the basis of recycling or ecologically friendly disposal capacity (among other green issues)
- Product and packaging design to facilitate return, recycling and safe disposal
- Visibility: the ability to access and view relevant logistics data, in order to manage the operation effectively
- Reverse logistical activities

The term 'network sourcing' is properly used in a technical sense to refer to a particular pattern of buyer-supplier interaction that has developed as a result of certain elements in the Japanese-style subcontracting system. Characteristics of network sourcing:

- Tiered supply structure
- Small number of direct suppliers
- High degree of asset specificity among suppliers
- Maximum buy, maximum make strategy
- Co-operative design and value engineering
- High degree of supplier innovation
- Close, long-term relations
- Rigorous supplier grading systems
- High level of supplier coordination by the customer company
- Significant supplier development efforts

The 'supplier base' is all the vendors that supply a given purchaser. One of the ways positive supplier relationships can be leveraged for supply chain improvement and competitiveness is by 'broadening supply'.

More commonly, strong collaborative supplier relationships are used to 'narrow supply', enabling purchases to be concentrated on a smaller group of developed and trusted supply partners. *Supplier base rationalisation* (or optimisation) is concerned with determining roughly how many suppliers the buying firm wants to do business with.

'The aim of supplier base optimisation is to leverage the buying power of an organisation with the smallest number of suppliers consistent with security of supplies and the need for high-quality goods and services at competitive prices.'

Risks of a narrow supplier base:

- Over-dependence on a few suppliers, in the event of supplier failure
- Supply disruption
- The loss of preferred suppliers' goodwill and co-operation
- Preferred suppliers growing complacent
- Being 'locked in' to long-term relationship and co-investment with suppliers who turn out to be under-performing or incompatible
- Missing out on seeking or utilising new or more competitive suppliers in the wider supply market.

OWN NOTES

OWN NOTES

CHAPTER 9

Managing Strategic Resources

Resources to support corporate strategy

Turning strategies into specific implementation plans – four elements:

- Identification of general strategic objectives
- Formulation of specific plans
- Resource allocation and budgeting – indicating how the plans are to be paid for
- Monitoring and control procedures.

The basic strategy implementation process

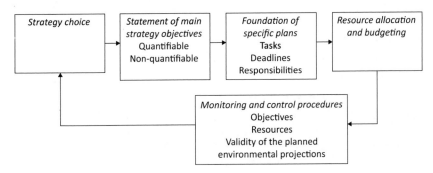

People as a resource

Human resource management (HRM) practitioners have long argued that people are the key to an organisation's success, added value and bottom line profitability. HRM is 'a strategic and coherent approach to the management of an organisation's most valued assets: the people working there who individually and collectively contribute to the achievement of its objectives.'

Key issues in effective use of the human resource through the **employment lifecycle.**

- Sourcing decisions (ie recruitment and selection, outsourcing)
- Resource development (ie appraisal and learning, training, improvement planning)

- Resource utilisation (ie goal-setting and performance assessment, etc)
- Resource retention and optimisation
- Resource disposal (ie managing employee exit, dismissals and redundancies)

Early organisation and management theories emphasised the extent to which the productivity and contribution of human resources is enabled or constrained by organisation structure. Johnson, Scholes and Whittington similarly argue that: 'as circumstances and strategies change, organisations may need to change... processes and relationships.' For example:

- Diversification and innovation strategies may require more collaborative, cross-functional or inter-organisational (supply chain) working.
- Competitive pressures may lead to strategies of focus on core competencies – which in turn may change internal relationships and processes.

Information as a resource

Three main areas where ICT has an impact on strategy: strategic capability, business models, and structures and management processes.

Strategic capability:

- Create product features valued by customers.
- Differentiate offerings and outperform competitors

Changing **business models**:

- Replacing paper-based processes with electronic processes
- Extending the functions that the business can offer

Structure and management processes – ICT:

- Supports new patterns of work organisation such as tele-working and networking
- Changes the nature, structure and management of work groups
- Enables simultaneous centralisation and decentralisation
- Replaces many of the decision-making, information-processing and supervisory functions of the middle line, facilitating delayering.

Management information tools:

- Databases and database management systems (DBMS)
- Decision support systems
- Management information systems

Enterprise resource planning (ERP) systems consolidate materials, manufacturing, logistics, supply chain, sales and marketing, finance and HR planning information into a single integrated management system: a single database able to offer 'real time' information for solving a range of business problems.

The benefits claimed for ERP include: integration and automation of many business processes; a general reduction in process costs; efficiency and flexibility gains;

standardisation and sharing of data and practices across the enterprise; generating and accessing decision support information on a 'real-time' basis; quicker response times and improved customer service; improved communication and data-sharing; and potentially improved supply chain management and relationships.

Tools supporting supply chain communication and data sharing:

- Electronic data interchange (EDI)
- The internet, extranets and intranets
- Mobile telecommunications and computing.

The development of procurement systems – a process of increasing integration:

- Independence
- Dependence
- Business integration
- Chain integration

Drivers for knowledge management:

- Business pressure for innovation
- Inter-organisational enterprises (eg mergers, takeovers)
- Networked organisations
- Increasingly complex products and services with a significant knowledge component
- Hyper-competitive global markets
- The digitisation of business environments and the ICT revolution
- Concerns about the loss of organisational knowledge

Technology as a resource

The general impact of technology on supply chains:

- Opening up new supply markets
- Changing business processes
- Raising supply chain capacity and productivity
- Improving communication and the visibility of information
- Changing the way that supply chains are organised and managed
- Freeing up procurement professionals' time
- Enhancing management information and feedback
- Supporting the development of supply chain relationships
- Reducing the risk of fraud

Drawbacks of technology:

- High capital investment and set-up costs
- High initial learning curve costs
- Reliability issues
- Compatibility issues
- Ethical issues
- Data security risks

9

Finance as a resource

Financial managers use a variety of **financial ratios** to evaluate financial performance.

- Profitability ratios
- Investment ratios
- Liquidity ratios
- Efficiency ratios

Procurement's contribution to value creation:

- Developing and managing supply chains and supplier relationships for value optimisation
- Value-chain repositioning
- Maximising share of the value in supply relationships

Sources of finance for private sector organisations:

- Retained profits
- Initial capital investment by the owners of the business or by venture capitalists
- Share capital
- Loan finance
- The sale of unneeded assets
- Government grants

Resource planning and control

Procurement and supply chain functions are nowadays encouraged to take a medium- to long-term view of materials requirements, and to put in place a variety of contractual arrangements which combine advantages for buyers and suppliers alike.

Appraising supply markets:

- Demand analysis
- Vendor analysis
- Market analysis

Performance targets focus on outputs such as revenue, profit, quality standards and other key performance indicators (KPIs).

Kaplan and Norton's balanced scorecard – four perspectives: financial; internal business processes; learning and growth; customer perspective.

OWN NOTES

OWN NOTES

CHAPTER 10

Managing Strategic Change

Types of strategic change

Triggers for change in the organisation or supply chain:

- Poor performance
- The presence of entrepreneurs, new senior management or other innovators
- Changes in, or re-ordering of, organisational goals, processes and structures
- Favourable changes experienced in the past
- Changes in knowledge or resources

Ten steps to building a compelling vision

Step 1 Assess the context: stakeholder needs and expectations; competitor strengths and responses and so on

Step 2 Look for trends: consider future needs and influences

Step 3 Think big: focus on key purposes and opportunities; create a challenge

Step 4 Think long term

Step 5 Envision: picture your desired future state vividly and in detail: 'dream' it.

Step 6 Check for passion: adjust the vision until it is meaningful, exciting, motivating

Step 7 Assess resource requirements: what competencies and resources will have to be sourced and mobilised to implement the vision

Step 8 Invite others in: involve people in the ideas, planning and implementation process

Step 9 Balance conviction and openness: believe in the rightness of the vision (for strength to lead and persevere) – but be open to ideas from others (for support and commitment)

Step 10 Stay objective: don't take criticism or rejection of your ideas personally: learn...

Competitive threats can offer a clear and compelling trigger for strategic change. In a radical case, competitive threat may result in a direct threat to business survival, creating a situation where immediate, rapid changes are required to increase market share and revenue and/or to reduce costs.

Benefits of **incremental (or evolutionary) change**

- It builds on existing skills, routines and beliefs in the organisation.
- It allows flexibility and responsiveness to environmental changes and feedback.
- It allows a continuous sense of progress, even through uncertainty and difficulty.
- It empowers employees.

10

Transformational (or revolutionary) change is often a reactive approach, responding to 'disruptive' change, crisis or the need for a completely new paradigm. It seeks to overthrow (or throw out) the *status quo* and introduce radical transformation in a relatively short period of time.

Balogun and Hope Hailey – four types of strategic change: adaptation; reconstruction; evolution; revolution.

Emergent and planned change:

- **Emergent change** is allowed to develop naturally, often from the bottom up, in response to environmental influences.
- **Planned change** involves deliberately formulated strategies and programmes for implementing change.

Analysing the change context

Contextual features which may influence strategic change programmes

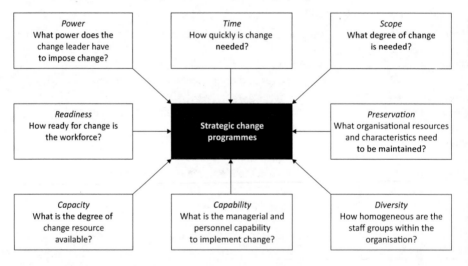

Force field analysis is a technique for identifying forces for and against change, in order to diagnose some of the change management problems that will need to be addressed, and some of the resources and dynamics available to support it. Force field analysis suggests a method of visualising or mapping the forces for and against change using directional arrows, the thicknesses of which represent the strength of each force.

The change equation: Change will be possible if:

$D \times V \times F > R$

In other words, if:

Dissatisfaction × Vision × First Steps is *greater* than Resistance.

Conditions favourable to change:

- Financial viability and stability
- Adaptable (or 'organic') organisation structures
- Good multi-directional communication systems, and systems for formal and informal negotiation and consultation
- Vision, leadership and support from senior management
- Supporting HR systems and procedures
- Supportive culture and attitudes

Barriers to organisational change

- Organisational focus
- Organisational structure
- Attitudes to security and risk
- Resources

The role of organisational culture

Hofstede summed up culture as 'the collective programming of the mind which distinguishes the members of one category of people from another'. It represents all the shared assumptions, beliefs, values, behavioural norms, symbols, rituals, stories and artefacts that make our society (or ethnic group, or organisation) distinctively 'us'.

Organisation culture is, in simple terms, the way in which a particular organisation does things: its distinctive 'climate' and 'style'. Structure and culture are often discussed together, as ways of describing an organisation and how it 'works': the formal arrangements are overlaid by a kind of collective 'personality'.

Elements in the cultural web: the paradigm; stories; routines and rituals; control systems; organisational structure; power structures; symbols.

10

Harrison/Handy's four cultural types

CULTURE	KEY FEATURES	ADVANTAGES/DISADVANTAGES
Power culture (Zeus: leader of the gods)	• Power centred in a key figure, owner or founder • Control through direct personal communication • Little formalisation, rules or procedures	• Suits small, entrepreneurial organisations of like-minded people • Enables the organisation to adapt quickly in response to change
Role culture (Apollo: god of order and rules)	• Classical, rational organisation (bureaucracy) • Formalised, impersonal: authority based on position, function; conformity to rules and procedures	• Efficient for large organisations in stable environments • Inability to change or innovate, due to rigidity
Task culture (Athena: goddess of wisdom and problem-solving)	• Management directed at outputs or results • Team-based organisation: horizontally structured, flexible • Valuing expertise, communication, collaboration	• Fosters results and customer focus Involves and empowers staff • Can be expensive (securing expertise, consensus decision-making)
Person culture (Dionysus: god of wine and song)	• Serves the interests of individuals: eg barristers working through chambers • Management function administrative and supportive, rather than directive (eg bursars or registrars)	• Supports individual talent and interests • Rare in practice

Overcoming strategic drift

In relatively stable environments, and for successful organisations, there will be periods of relative continuity, during which core strategy continues more or less unchanged, or changes only incrementally. There are a number of reasons why an organisation might only pursue incremental change, leading to strategic drift. Managers may be:

- Aligning the organisation's strategy incrementally to an environment which is itself only changing gradually
- Reluctant to depart from established approaches
- Relying on core competencies
- Committed to long-term value-adding relationships
- Committed to an approach of logical incrementalism

Symptoms of strategic drift:

- Complacency, and the repression of questioning and challenge
- A conservative culture
- An inward focus
- Widespread inertia and resistance to change
- Deteriorating business performance.

Overcoming resistance to change

Four factors affecting the individual's **response to change**: facts; beliefs; feelings; values.

Reactions to proposed changes:

- Acceptance: enthusiastic espousal, willing cooperation, grudging cooperation or resigned compliance
- Indifference: apathy, lack of interest, inaction
- Passive resistance
- Active resistance

Reasons for individual and organisational resistance to change

INDIVIDUAL RESISTANCE	ORGANISATIONAL RESISTANCE
Selective perception, leading to biased views of the situation	Organisational culture: strong norms and values establishing the *status quo*
Habit, providing ease, comfort and security	A desire to maintain stability and predictability (especially in bureaucratic organisations)
Inconvenience, loss of control or reduced freedom of action	Resource requirements and priorities (economic feasibility, asset specificity)
Economic implications of change for pay, rewards or job security	Past and existing contracts and agreements, constraining changes in behaviour (eg long-term supplier contracts)
Nostalgia: value and security in the past, tradition, 'tried and tested' ways	Threats to the power or influence of interest groups (protecting functional territory or managerial power, say)
Fear of the unknown and insecurity	Blaming culture (discouraging experimentation) or deference culture (discouraging intiative).

Six approaches to overcoming resistance to change:

- Education and communication
- Participation and involvement
- Facilitation and support
- Negotiation and agreement
- Manipulation and co-optation
- Explicit and implicit coercion

10

Managing strategic change

Lewin and Schein's three-step model for changing human behaviour:

The planned change (unfreeze-change-refreeze) model

Why change programmes fail:

Ritualisation of change	Continual incremental change programmes come to be seen as empty rituals, rather than meaningful changes
Hijacked processes	Leaders or units hijack change efforts in order to serve their own agendas (eg downsizing, power enhancement)
Erosion	The programme is overtaken by other events and priorities emerging in the organisation: momentum is lost or diverted
Reinvention	The attempted change is reinterpreted through the lens of the old culture, which simply reinforces the status quo (the organisation convinces itself it's 'already doing that')
Ivory tower change	Change driven by senior or external agents is perceived to be out of touch with the realities of the market, losing credibility
Inattention to symbols	Change agents fail to link the 'big messages' about change to organisational values and symbols. Change may be seen as irrelevant – or the wrong message (eg blame) may be given.
Uncontrolled/unco-ordinated effort	New practices are inconsistent with the thrust of change as understood by people in the organisation, creating lack of coherence
Behavioural compliance	People comply with changes, without commitment: the programme may look successful, but the changes may not be effective or lasting

Strategic change roles

Change agents are individuals or teams who are appointed or empowered to drive a change programme: change programme or project managers, external change management consultants, and functional managers pursuing change objectives.

Advantages of external change agents:

- They are more likely to be objective and dispassionate.
- They may better represent the interests of other stakeholders in the change process and outcomes.
- They are better able to ask questions and perform analyses which challenge the *status quo* and its constraints, and broaden the range of options.
- They may have technical expertise.
- They are dedicated to the change programme.
- They represent a significant, focused investment in change.

OWN NOTES

OWN NOTES